# Eleven Poems

# and

# One Story

## By Rajko Igić

Second Edition

Biographical Publishing Company
Prospect, Connecticut

# Eleven Poems and One Story

## Second Edition

Published by:

Biographical Publishing Company
35 Clark Hill Road
Prospect, CT 06712-1011
Phone: 203-758-3661 Fax: 208-247-1493
e-mail: biopub@aol.com

PRINTED IN THE UNITED STATES OF AMERICA

Library of Congress Cataloging-in-Publication Data

Igić, Rajko, 1937-
Eleven poems and one story / by Rajko Igić ; [Borka Tomljenović, translator ; George Cermak, illustrator].-- 2nd ed. p. cm. 1.
Igić, Rajko, 1937---Originals and translations into English. I. Title: 11 poems and 1 story. II. Tomljenović, Borka, 1917- III. Cermak, George, 1916-
IV. Title.
PG1419.19.G53 E44
2001 891.8'216--dc21
2001095381
ISBN 1929882211

# Table of Contents

# List of Illustrations

# Editor's Note

The new edition of this book includes the same poems and story from the First Edition with a few improvements in the Glossary and Notes. Also, some readers were interested in the illustration titles. These titles were kindly provided by George Cermak and are found in the List of Illustrations.

John Guevin                                    August 31, 2001

# Acknowledgments

This collection includes my poems written in the last two years. A few of the poems I wrote in English and the others were written in the Serbo-Croatian language. The latter were kindly translated by Ms. Borka Tomljenović, Ann Arbor, MI. I have reworked some of the translations to their present form. Dr. Dragan Milivojević, Norman, OK, prepared the Introduction. I would like to thank George Cermak, Evanston, IL, for his drawings, Michelle Hartnett, Chicago, IL, who helped me to prepare the final version of the manuscript, and Linda Teplitz, Palos Park, IL, and Sonja Nikčević, Belgrade, Yugoslavia, for their suggestions. Luba Stojiljković, Chicago, IL, helped us to transmit illustrations electronically to the editor. The poem "Are We Inferior to Dolphins" was published in the book <u>A Forgotten Paradise</u> (The International Library of Poetry, Owings Mills, 2000; p.207) and several medical journals. Mr. Hasan Fazlić, Sarajevo, Bosnia and Herzegovina, prepared the cartoon for my book <u>Nova slovarica</u> (Univerzal, Tuzla) and it is shown on the front cover in this book.

Chicago, August 2001                                                              R. I.

A Scientist and a Poet

The two professions of scientist and poet are seldom combined in our modern world of overspecialization. In our world, human beings know more and more about less and less in such a way that scientists in the same field can hardly talk and understand each other's research. It didn't used to be that way. Chekhov was a medical doctor and that was his nominal profession, but his achievements in literature vastly overreached his modest medical accomplishments. So it is refreshing and surprising to hear about a person who is able to combine successfully in this day and age what is usually kept apart — a scientific career and a poetical activity.

The two sides of the poet — the scientific and the poetic — live uncomfortably with each other. As a scientist, the author should be optimistic and a believer that science can cure all human ills, that it will bring progress and success and a better life, but as a poet, the author feels differently. His life experience has taught him what science overlooks and ignores: the senselessness of war, the loss of his national identity and his country, the emigration and new beginning in another country and language.

The collection of poems follows a chronological pattern. It starts with childhood in his native Yugoslavia and ends with his stay in the United States. This transition does not appear, as it is usually portrayed in our citizenship posters, as happiness and exhilaration in settling in a prosperous and free country, because a man does not live by bread alone. As time progresses, it brings with it a series of losses. In the poem "Spring," the loss of his carefree childhood takes place and a hint of violence and sacrifice is described with a snake devouring a frog. Later, in the Balkans, it will be people who will "devour" each other. In the poem "For my Father" the life of an honest and hardworking person is portrayed who, in spite of all his efforts, does not achieve his goals and remains the victim of social upheaval over which he has no control. His son dreams of a better world in the aftermath of the world war, of brotherhood and unity, the slogans of the new regime which sound noble and fair, of new opportunities in education which were not open to his father. This dream turned out to be a deception phrased innocently by his son. "At the tender age of seven, my son Boris asked me: "Papa, why are we still in the Balkans?" (Prophesy). The author in the poem "The Price of Progress" points out the hollowness of governmental slogans: "I was educated in socialism/and for a long time I didn't know about elitism/ because we were taught that life is best/if

10

our ideal is Marx and Communism/When Fulbright showed me another world . . ." (The reference is to the Fulbright grant which enabled the author to do research in the United States.) Just like his father, the author had an experience of another war. This time it may be even more savage than the one proceeding it, because it was a civil war and the war in which the author lost his country.

There are a few poems in the collection which stand apart from their subject matter. "The Serbs and Heaven" is the author's intention to provide a historical perspective for the much maligned Serbs in the

wake of the recent war in the region: "The Serbs stood bravely in the Balkans/ Defending the borders of the West/ They saved Europe from the Turks." The sub-text of the poem is that this sacrificial gesture has not been honored and appreciated by the Western powers in view of their war inflicted on Yugoslavia. In "A Ballad About a Mediterranean Fisherman" the conflict between the scientist and the poet comes to a head with the poet taking the upper hand. The old fisherman believes that there is a time for making love and there is a time for foreswearing it. Science in the form of Viagra-like products should desist from interfering with the natural cycle of life.

The poem "Winter" sums up the general reflective mood of this poetical collection. The poet walks in the blizzard and the death of nature in its midst causes him to think about death, passage of time and the fate of human beings. Death of the people who freeze in the cold is described as ". . . the realm of a magic dream," and life in a communal shelter is described as ". . . the hell of living." Death seems to be preferable to the misery of living. He thinks about his grandfather and his mother who, when they were in their nineties, always felt cold even in the heat of the midsummer's day, and he thinks of ". . . our own transitions that lead our bodies into irretrievable coldness." Similar in content and in tone is the poem "Life Passes Away" in which the poet compares two kinds of living heritage. The one is heroic, of Joan of Arc, Byron, Lorca and Martin Luther King and other ordinary human beings who ". . . leave a mark . . . a short or long memory behind . . ." Opposed to this doomsday feeling is the hope of a better future in the poem "*Quo vadis*, Humanity?" "We are waiting for the idea that will lead us to permanent peace and salvation of humanity." How long should we wait?

After reading this collection, I came to believe that Dr. Igić has a poet's sensibility and feelings in a scientific mind. Each occupies its own sphere, but when they clash in his poetry, it is the former that prevails.


Dragan Milivojević, Ph.D.

Professor Emeritus, University of Oklahoma

Two Seasons

# Spring

Days get longer, and the sun gets warmer,
Nature wakes up and St. Ivan's gardens, meadows
And fields are in haste to put on green attire.

The war has recently ended, and freedom has come
Together with the help provided by UNRRA.
We put on that strangely cut suit for school,
But we are still without shoes. Only a few days ago,
We took off our clumsy wooden clogs,
And are now wearing comfortable felt slippers
Suitable for shooting the ball
Until it gets warm enough to play barefoot.

Newly arrived swallows have enriched the village fauna,
Closely followed by other familiar migratory birds,
Two huge storks. They settled down in the big nest
Perched on the chimney of Uncle Laza's house,
Where we, first graders and even older children, used to stop
When returning from school.

We are taught religion by Bajazet, the bearded
And dignified village priest; we don't pay much
Attention to him until he declares that in a day
Or two we shall have to go to *Vrbica*.

We set out from our school and cross a vast
And flowery field, Podbara, dotted with wild
Red poppies and flowers of different colors,
Which compete with and look down upon
The monotonously green grass.

We cross the Jegrička, still full of water,
And arrive at the field which only a few months ago
Served as a Russian army airbase.

There are no planes there any more,
Which we, excited, followed when they left on a mission
And returned with an occasional acrobatic figure.
We felt sad that we could no longer hear their noise,
Because all the boys were ready,
Even before growing up, to become pilots.

Our teacher, Milena, a lovely young woman,
Cuts for us willow twigs, and gives one to each,
When suddenly we hear cries: "Snake, snake!"

I turn round and see it stretched out, hissing and staring
At a small frog which, transfixed, remains motionless.
In a second or two the trophy is won, but all night I cried,
Feeling sorry for the frog, repeating to myself:
"Why didn't you jump and escape that villain?"

Novi Sad, May 2000

## Winter

For a week, Chicago has been in the grips of a strong wind
which, two days ago, ushered in a polar cold and deep snow,
compelling citizens to seek protection by warm hearths.

It is Sunday. Rare pedestrians and cars can hardly find
their way through piles of snow; the distances have become
longer, if you can cover them at all.

I am walking to the subway, pushing my way beside
the snowbound cars, as I am going along to cover
the distance of three blocks, twice I had to briefly
take shelter to regain some warmth.

The little park in front of the hospital is quite impenetrable,
and the monument with Louis Pasteur's message is
completely covered with snow.
The blizzard has taken his noble words prisoner.

Winter has already cleared the streets of homeless citizens
who sleep out-of-doors even in frosty weather.
Where are they now, and where is their home
in this bitter cold? Some have been moved by social workers
to a communal shelter, where these freedom-loving people
reluctantly go, accepting life on the street rather than
dwelling in the hell of living.

Some, I thought, perhaps have been already transferred
by this cold weather into the realm of a magic dream,
before their bodies have turned into ice.

While I am walking beside this little park, making a path
in the deep snow, a touch of sadness descends upon me
as I thought of our grandfather, Did, and my mother,
who, in their nineties, felt cold even in midsummer.

Thus, the cyclic seasonal changes of nature
have reminded me, in the dead of the winter, of our own
transitions that lead our bodies into irretrievable coldness.

Chicago, December 2000

My Father and My Sons

# For My Father

It is a long time, Father, that you are not with us,
but I often think of you, and wish to build you
a monument with these words.

You did not remember your Mother,
and you lost your Father when you were five.
Others brought you up, and an alien army
sent you to the Carpathians to fight.
You fled, but were returned to an attack detachment;
your wounds were healed by the peasant's family
whose language you did not understand.
To build our house and bring up five of us,
you worked hard and toiled on other people's fields.
For a while you were a foreign worker, brought
the first bike into our village, and bought an old thresher.
You defeated a champion wrestler, you supported the poor,
and you were even sung about, but you couldn't pass
in crooked elections.

We were overjoyed when, after four years
of forced labor, you returned from Germany.
You found us in poverty, but alive.
"Volksdeutschers" took our horses when they
fled Bačka, and I grieved for the dappled horse, Laci,
until you bought me another horse. You set records
in harvest yields, you bought land, and sent me to college.

You yourself hardly had any schooling;
you were self-taught, and subscribed to magazines.
You surveyed the St. Ivan area during the agrarian reform,
and solved for me difficult arithmetical problems.
You refused to accept a position in Tito's Yugoslavia,
because you believed in God and went to church.

Thank you for bringing me up with love, but strictly,
for advising me to keep away from land and collective farms,
for telling me that knowledge is a treasure that
offers great satisfaction, and that only knowledge
can leave a credible mark.

I was wrong, Father, when I asked you to remove
St. Nicholas' icon so that I would not be ashamed before
my atheist colleagues. That is why I carried it across the
ocean to remember you and all our ancestors who honored
this great Christian and observed his day with decorum.

Sombor, May 2000

# Prophesy

At the tender age of seven,
my son Boris asked me:
"Papa, why are we still in the Balkans?"

Seven years have passed since then,
and he, I, and all our family are now
on the other side of the world, in exile,
far away from the Balkans.

This childish question, which at the time
was published by the "Jež," appears to me today
like a cruel prediction.

Igalo, June 2000

# Fate

When Petar, my elder son,
became a top basketball player,
like an ear of grain,
he became mature before his time.

I took him with me on a study tour
to learn the language and see the world,
but then I lost him like a culled flower.
He wished to remain in the country
of the top basketball players,
although it was not to my taste.

Just as the wind sways a young plant
so the joint of an athlete becomes loose,
and then he embarks upon an academic career.

San Diego, April 2000

Can We Prevent War?

# Dream

Last night I dreamed that I was declaring war
On all the armies on this planet.
"I have no fear of guns, bombs or rockets.
I have no army; words are my weapons."

I was appealing to unarmed masses to seek justice,
Not to be afraid of any army,
And I was crying out: "Words are our weapons!"

To the armed I sent word to abandon guns:
"Soldiers, beware of your unarmed brethren,
Because the word of the people is the strongest weapon!"

With a start, I woke up from this century's last night
Feeling unhappy that on this planet justice must wait.
Will the time ever come when sober reality
Will wake up masses from their profound sleep?

Chicago, January 2001

# Are We Inferior to Dolphins

Chilean brother Pablo composed
A message that the majority did not get.
"O beautiful is this planet,
I came to live in this world."

"For a formula to prevent every unnecessary tomb,
To be secure as when sheltered in the womb,
A man doesn't need help of smart dolphin's steer —"
Exclaims Dudley, my distinguished peer.

Thus, an intellectual is forced to choose
The ideal of altruism or selfishness,
And if the selection is deadly wrong,
To a war-free era we will never belong.

My dear reader and distinguished friend,
Every war represents humanity's end.

Chicago, May 1999


# The Serbs and Heaven

To understand an Orthodox person,
Listen to this liturgy, the art of arts,
And look at the Patron Saint's icon
In the home of Serbian peasants.

The Serbs stood bravely in the Balkans,
Defending the borders of the West.
They saved Europe from the Turks
And preserved their ancient Christianity.

Was King Stefan the First confused
When he ignored the well-trodden path
And proudly refused the Pope's offer,
Preferring Heaven for the Serbs' destination?

If heaven on Earth is your vision,
You will misread Tsar Lazar and his Legion,
Who rather chose the Earth to leave
Than to become a Turkish captive.

Chicago, May 1999

# *Quo vadis,* Humanity?

Man first had an idea to draw something,
then he sought a way to realize it.
The famous drawings of bison were probably first
drawn on sand, and then with charcoal or some
better material on the walls of the cave.

Ideas led to paintings, written records, and
various objects in order to express beauty, joy,
fear, belief, thought, and suffering.
Men with ideas became painters, poets, warriors,
founders of religions, and philosophers.

Men of practice invented clothes, footwear, bread,
medicines, boat and ship, wheel, engine, microscope,
aircraft, genetic manipulations, computer, and space craft.
Life became easier, longer and more interesting, and men
multiplied and spread all over the world.

Artists and humanists strive to understand man,
while scientists help us to better know the physical and
biological world, from atom and molecule to universe.
They both are motivated by curiosity, a distinctive feature
of man. As Garfield stated, works of Homer, Plato, writers
of the Bible, Shakespeare, Goethe, Pushkin, Mozart, Marx,
and other great men have stimulated modern humanists
and all those that would like to know man, whereas scientists
look for support in their  predecessors.

With every two steps forward, humanity takes
one to two steps toward barbarity.
Man killed man with hands, or by drowning, with stone or
knife, and carried out mass killing by fire, gun, bomb,
concentration camp, atomic bomb, missile, and economic
blockade. Now is the turn of anti-missiles, shelters in
satellites and other planets — cosmic war.

Will the end of humanity be brought about by our cruelty?
Will humanists and scientists help us to understand
and improve our behavior, which directs us to inhumane acts?
We are waiting for the idea that will lead us to permanent
peace and the salvation of humanity.

Chicago, September 2000

Solitude and Society

# The Price of Progress

I was educated in Socialism
And for a long time I didn't know about elitism,
Because we were taught that life is best
If our ideal is Marx and Communism.

When Fulbright showed me a different world,
I realized that life could be beautiful
In a backward country, according Tito, which
Was led by an elite.

Having become familiar with that different order,
I concluded that prosperity, too, must be paid for,
And it is clear who will have the bad luck
To pay the highest bill in the society.


San Diego, April 2000

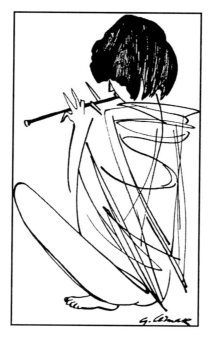

# Life Passes Away

You spend years in learning, working,
in pleasure and suffering...
You grow frailer.
Your friends leave you, disappear,
Or simply die.

If you have gone far away,
Your memories often turn to your homeland,
And when they begin to fade,
You long to return and revive them.

With impatience you wait for your enemies to leave;
Secretly hoping for it, you avoid them.
As a sign of protest, you go out into the streets
Or take up arms.

Sometimes the end itself, like that of Joan of Arc,
Byron, Lorca or Martin Luther King,
Generates numerous elegies and eternal memory
As a tribute to a heroic life and a tragic end.

We live to leave a mark —
To leave a short or long memory behind.
Passing away, we make room for those who are coming.

Brussels National Airport, May 2000

# A Ballad About a Mediterranean Fisherman

When summer came, all of us from the former Yugoslavia flocked to the Adriatic. It was in agreement with the popular song "The Blue Adriatic is undulating while the working class is resting." We took possession of the coast and of the numerous islands of the beautiful and peaceful sea that once belonged to all of us.

One summer, I came with my family to the island of Hvar or Pharos as the ancient Greeks had called it. We inhaled deeply the balmy island air fraught with the ethereal oils of the Mediterranean plants. It was pleasant to observe how the night sky drew near. Time passed slowly.

For our residence, we chose Stari Grad, the home city of the famous poet, Petar Hektorović, and remembered that he showed enthusiasm for the folk poetry of South Slavs more than two centuries before Goethe, Byron, Mérimée, Petoefi, Mickiewicz, and Pushkin discovered the beauty of our "folk" literature. Our bard spent many days with the fishermen at sea, where he recognized the value of this poetry and he recorded several poems that were transmitted orally by generations of illiterate poets.

For three days I rested, swimming and enjoying the dishes of fish and vegetables prepared with olive oil. With a lady journalist from Bonn I had long conversations, accompanied by good Dalmatian wine. On the fourth day, two local people came to ask me if I could come to see their relative who would be a hundred years old in several days, if he lived through his present illness. I asked them how they had learned about me, and they said that the youngest son of the ill person was a retired doctor and lived inland. They said that he had heard that I was here, and he thought that, as a professor, I would be a most suitable person to examine his father.

The fishermen's settlement was huddled between a hill and the narrow bay dotted with fishermen's boats. A very narrow street leading to the patient's home brought us first to a small square in front of the church. Barba's crisis of last night was already over. His breathing, resembling a death rattle during the night that scared his caretakers, was almost normal. I enquired about his health problems, examined him and prescribed medications.

A member of his family provided me with a basin, a jug of water, a bar of soap and a towel to wash my hands. They offered me fresh figs and coffee. The patient dozed off. In the meantime, I learned that as a young man Barba had spent more than ten years working in America, and as soon as the old man awoke, I began to talk to him in English.

In excellent English, he told me how he traveled to America as a stowaway at the end of the 19th century. Still a teenager, he then went to Chicago, where he found a job, and later returned to Dalmatia once he had earned enough money. Upon return, he bought his present house, a large fishing boat, got married, and had three sons. I noticed that our conversation in English had cheered him up.

It is not often that you can speak with a near centenarian of a mind seemingly clearer than my own. Therefore, as soon as I found out that none of the members of his household spoke English, I carefully put to him a delicate question. My intention was to learn how long he had been sexually active.

"The last time I was with a woman, I was 79 years old. I was a widower, and I had an affair with a widow from my neighborhood who was thirty

years younger than I. For ten years and three months, we met secretly, as we could not marry because of her children and mine."

"Where could you meet in this settlement which is so closely knit that two people can hardly pass each other?" I asked. "Do you see the attic where the laundry is dried?" He pointed it out to me through the window. "I would take some food and *bevanda* with me and wait for her there for an hour or so."

"Well? And what happened after ten years?" I asked. "My dear companion suddenly fell ill with pneumonia and was dead in two weeks," replied Barba in a trembling voice and with tears in his eyes. "She has taken our secret to her grave, and now I am giving it away to you. Almighty God, forgive me!"

I wanted to find out from this clear-minded old man what life is like once sexual pleasures are over. "You become somehow calmer, free from yourself, your memories become more important, and you get strength to live because of these memories," concluded Barba.

Today, when I listen to loud advertisements for the prolonging and restoring of sexual drive far beyond the age that nature has ordained for us, I wonder whether it is necessary to curtail the period of peace and unique freedom at the end of the life of a human male. "Suo tempore," as the old Romans used to say. "There is a time for everything."

Chicago, March 2000

# Glossary and Notes

**UNRRA** — United Nations Relief and Rehabilitation Administration, organization founded in 1943 during World War II to give aid to areas liberated from the Axis powers. The parcels we received in Despotovo came from the USA and the contents included clothes, some canned food and a pack of cigarettes. Due to the availability of cigarettes, many children started to smoke. Thus, when I was seven I smoked two cigarettes, one after the other, and became intoxicated. My parents and Dr. Arkadije Zajčev, our physician, did not know what was the nature of my sickness, but I have never smoked again.

**The Willow Feast** [in Serbian, Vrbica] — is observed on the last Saturday, Lazarus' Day, before Easter. This holiday is celebrated with great solemnity as a kind of children's holiday.

**Jegrička** — is a small river in Bačka, the northwestern part of Vojvodina. This river collects water from a huge part of this plain and brings it to the Tisa River. Jegrička does not have a permanent origin and mouth. During the summer, the river in Despotovo is shallow and one can easily cross it on foot. Its banks are overgrown with goat willow, elder and poplar trees. At all times this river serves for drainage and irrigation. However, it has recently become incorporated into the modern system of canals for irrigation that were dug through Vojvodina.

**Louis Pasteur's message** — In 1928, the people of Chicago erected in front of Cook County Hospital a monument to Louis Pasteur. The following words of this "servant of humanity" are written on the monument: "One doesn't ask of one who suffers: What is your country and what is your religion? One merely says, you suffer, this is enough for me, you belong to me and I shall help you." Today, as always, in Cook County Hospital every citizen gets necessary medical treatment. Poor people, who do not have health insurance, get all necessary medical attention free of charge. I am privileged to work in this hospital that truly belongs to the people of Chicago.

**Did** — Petar Munitić, father of my wife Danica, from Grabovac, Dalmatia. His children, grandchildren, and all his family called him Did. In the Dalmatian dialect it means grandfather.

**Volksdeutscher** [German] — A German who is born and lives in a foreign country. In Vojvodina, the northern part of Serbia, Germans immigrated in the 1880s. They lived in separate settlements or they joined villages and towns where local Serbian populations lived. Approximately ten percent of Germans lived in Despotovo before WWII. Most of them did not have their own land; they worked for rich Germans in Torza, a village four miles away. Because these local Germans supported Hitler, most of them did not want to wait for the Russians and Tito's partisans to come and they fled to Austria and Germany, just a few weeks before Vojvodina was liberated. The majority of these local Germans did not have automobiles or tractors; they confiscated horses and carriages from the local Serbs.

**The Carpathian Mountains**— are part of the great mountain system of Central Europe. The Carpathians are an extension of the mountain range which includes the Alps, but the Carpathian peaks are generally lower than the Alps. During WWI, the Austro-Hungarian forces fought with the Russian forces. Because Vojvodina was part of Austria-Hungary, its citizens were obliged to serve in the national service. Adult males from Despotovo, from 18 to 60 years of age, were mobilized to the army and the majority of them were sent to the Eastern Front in the Carpathian Mountains to fight against the Russians, their brothers. As most of them did not like to fight, some deserted or even went over to the Russian side. During WWI, at the Eastern Front, in a series of campaigns led by the German commander von Hindenburg, around the swampy Masurian Lakes, Russian armies lost more than 300,000 men. But in Galicia, the Russians killed and wounded more than 250,000 Austrian troops, and captured 100,000 others in the Battle of Lemberg, now Lvov, Ukraine.

**St. Ivan** — An Austro-Hungarian name for Despotovo, now with 3,000 inhabitants. St. Ivan frequently changed its name. Between WWI and WWII, it became Despot Sveti-Ivan. (Despot — the title for Byzantine or Ottoman Vassal Ruler, and a bishop of the Orthodox Church. Also, tyrant.) When the Russians came, it was named Vasiljevo, after their captain who was the first who entered the village. In 1948, when Yugoslavia broke its relationship with the USSR, the place got its present name, Despotovo.

**Jež** (Hedgehog)— a magazine for humor and satire that is published in Belgrade.

**Pablo** — Pablo Neruda, the 1971 Nobel Prize-winning Chilean poet.

**Dudley** — Dudley Herschbach, the 1986 Nobel Prize-winning US Scientist. He was inspired by Leo Szilard's book, <u>The Voice of Dolphins</u>. Herschbach was fascinated by the workings of dolphin society, particularly how these animals work together. If a dolphin becomes unconscious or injured, others rush to its aid and float it to the surface where it can breathe just like other mammals. Otherwise, the injured animal would drown. Further, the dolphins have a communication system that links large herds and enables them to react as if possessed with a "group mind." Herschbach suggests that if we could think like dolphins, we would understand that problems involving differences in gender, race, religion, political persuasion, or national identity would recede when confronted by our common humanity. Perhaps the behavior of dolphins could teach us to enlarge our own perspective and to enhance our own capabilities. And perhaps this insight might help to solve many of the problems we humans regard as insoluble (D. Herschbach, *Harvard Magazine*, Jan-Feb 1993, 57-59).

**Icon (Ikona)** [Greek] — a conventional religious image painted by an artist on a piece of wooden panel, linen or — rarely — glass and used in devotions of Eastern Christianity. Each Serbian family celebrates a patron saint, such as St. Nicholas, St. John, St. George, etc. Perhaps this tradition originates from the 9th century when their pagan festivities were converted to this unique Christian heritage. Every Serbian home keeps an icon of its saint in the sitting room.

**Fresco, pl. frescoes or frescos** [Italian] — The art or technique of painting on a freshly spread, moist surface of plaster with color ground up in water or lime water mixture.

The most distinctive feature of Serbian medieval art is its frescoes. These frescoes reflect well the time and the society in which they were created. Frescoes, which are painted on walls, are as durable as mosaics, and in spite of the ravages of time and especially those inflicted by men, many have survived in their original beauty. Although Byzantine by origin, Serbian frescoes have achieved a measure of originality, which distinguishes them from their original models, notably by the display of emotions and feelings unusual for Byzantine frescoes. Thus, these frescoes anticipate by a century some methods of treatment once thought original to Duccio and Giotto.

**King Stefan the First-Crowned** (ruled from 1196 to 1228) — was the son of grand župan, Stefan Nemanja (ruled from 1168 to 1196), the founder of Serbia's medieval dynasty which governed the Serbian kingdom for 200 years.

For a time King Stefan broke his ties with Byzantium and turned to the West, to Venice and Rome, to seek help against invading Bulgarians and Hungarians. He was twice crowned: in 1217 by a crown of Pope Honorius III and in 1220 by his younger brother, Sava. The Pope sought to convert the Serbs to Catholicism, but King Stefan did not forsake his Orthodoxy thanks to his brother Rastko, who had become a monk and assumed the name of Sava. Sava became one of Serbia's most revered saints. Thanks to him, the Serbian Church was elevated to the status of an autocephalous bishopric. This event sealed the destiny of the Serbs for it solidified ties with Eastern Orthodoxy and influenced the course of Serbian history for centuries to come.

**Tsar Lazar** — was the leader of Slav forces at the battle of Kosovo in 1389. He was killed on the field together with the Turkish sultan, Murad. However, the Turkish Empire soon conquered all Serbian lands and their rule lasted for five centuries.

**Quo vadis?** [Latin] — "Where are you going?" According to a legend, this is the question that St. Peter asked Christ whom he met when he was fleeing Rome. The Quo Vadis church was erected on that spot on Via Apia. Also, a historical novel by Henryk Sienkiewicz, published in 1895, has such a name.

**Fulbright** — The Fulbright Program was established in 1946 under congressional legislation introduced by Senator J. William Fulbright of Arkansas. This program is designed to "increase mutual understanding between the people of the United States and the people of other countries." One of many programs within the Fulbright Program, the Visiting Scholar Program awards grants to foreign scholars and professionals to come to the United States to lecture and conduct postdoctoral research. Nearly 700 scholars come annually to the States. I was a Fulbright fellow from 1970 to1972 at the Department of Pharmacology, University of Oklahoma, Oklahoma City.

**Garfield** — Dr. Eugene Garfield, Philadelphia, PA, is the father of modern information science.

**Petar Hektorović** (1487-1582) — a Croatian Renaissance poet and Latin scholar. He lived in the Tvrdalj castle, Stari Grad, Hvar Island, Dalmatia. He designed the castle and surrounding landscape himself. Due to the circumstances, a long, closed facade of the castle is facing the sea. The centerpiece of the building is the fish-pool, enclosed by an arcaded terrace. As his inscriptions say, he wanted to accommodate himself and his friends in this mansion, but also it served as a stronghold for his family and all the citizens of Stari Grad in the case of a Turkish invasion of the island. The eastern part of Tvrdalj was used to accept the poor people and for travelers. His philosophy of life is reflected in his words: "Know that neither riches nor world fame nor beauty or age can save you, for death seizes everything." While he was on a three-day excursion to the sea in 1555, he recorded six folk songs of exceptional beauty. Hektorović published them in his travelogue in verse, "Fishermen and Fishermen's Conversation" (Venice, 1568). He stated that the fishermen "in their free time" entertained him by singing folk songs "in Serbian style." Among them was "The Death of the Mother of the Jugovići," one of the poems in which the collective memory of the people describes the events connected with the battle of Kosovo, 1389, an event of paramount importance in the history of the South Slavs, especially the Serbs.

**Barba** — uncle, an old man. Along the Adriatic coast in the former Yugoslavia, especially in Dalmatia, an elderly man is addressed as "barba." Barba in Latin means beard.

**Dubrovnik** — City and port in South Croatia on the Adriatic Sea. According to Rebecca West (*Black Lamb and Grey Falcon*, New York: Penguin, 1994, p.230), it was called Ragusa until it became part of Yugoslavia. The name was changed, although it is pure Illyrian, because it sounded Italian. For centuries, this town was an independent state, not a protectorate. It never fell under the rule of the Turks, the Venetians, or the Hungarians. Though Dubrovnik was a republic located on a tiny peninsula only a half mile across, it was for a long period a great economic empire. Now a city, Dubrovnik is exquisite, perhaps the most beautiful city I have ever seen. When I lived in Bosnia, I used to visit Dubrovnik several times a year to participate in various scientific or cultural gatherings, to rest, to show its beauty to my foreign guests, or simply to enjoy this marvelous city.

# Map Showing Yugoslav States

Places in former Yugoslavia where the author lived, studied, and/or worked as a physician are underlined. The author spent his summer vacations in his house in Rukavac, a small fishing village on Vis Island. These places are now in three separate countries.

# About the Author

Rajko Igić was born in Despotovo, Yugoslavia. He studied medicine at the universities of Sarajevo and Belgrade and worked for several years as a physician in Sombor and Kucura, Vojvodina. In 1967 he moved to Sarajevo. Dr. Igić was founder and head of the Department of Pharmacology at the University of Tuzla from 1978 to 1992 and director of the Department of Scientific, Cultural, Technical, and Educational International Exchange for the Republic of Bosnia and Herzegovina in Sarajevo from 1990 to 1992. He published numerous scientific papers, several textbooks for medical students, and books, including "Nova Slovarica" (Univerzal, Tuzla, 1987). In 1985, he devised a combined alphabet, Slavica, to be used instead of two existing alphabets for Serbian or Croatian language. His intention was to bring about a closer association among the four nationalities in the Yugoslav area, "who speak practically one language, but write in two different alphabets."

As a medical student, the author voluntarily spent three summer vacations in Tremnik, Anska Reka, and Kumanovo, Republic of Macedonia, building the Brotherhood and Unity Highway. In 1961, he led a group of 120 medical students from the University of Belgrade, and they continued the building of this highway, dreaming of a better world. Dr. Igić started an international campaign of medical students "January 31st— A Day Without a Cigarette" that in several years contributed to a slight decrease in smoking prevalence among the citizens in the former Yugoslavia, and several European countries. The World Heath Organization appreciated this preventive activity in 1991 and invited 40 students from Tuzla to a special meeting in Geneva, Switzerland.

The civil war in Yugoslavia forced him to leave Bosnia in May, 1992. For a short time, he stayed in Sombor and Novi Sad, and in 1993 he moved to the United States of America. In his free time, he has studied the effect of the war in Yugoslavia on scientific publication. Igić published his ideas on war prevention in various medical journals and other publications, including the *Scientist, Scientometrics, Chicago Tribune, New York Times,* and *European.*

# About the Translator

Borka Tomljenović left Yugoslavia in 1992, and came to live with her daughter in Ann Arbor, MI, where she works at the International Center of the University of Michigan. Since she immigrated in the USA, she has published three books: <u>Bosnian Counterpoint</u>, <u>Neither on the Earth nor in the Sky</u>, and <u>Requiem for Yugoslavia</u>. These cover the period between 1941 and 1991 in which she has related the events that have changed the inter-ethnic and personal relations in her former homeland.

# About the Illustrator

George Cermak lives in Evanston, IL. After graduation from the Royal Academy of Arts, Belgrade, Mr. Cermak was selected by Maurice de Vlaminck to be his student in the Ecolle des Beaux Arts, Paris, France. Mr. Cermak had many art exhibitions in the USA and various European countries. He also taught art at several universities.